"WOW!! IF YOU'VE EV[...] housesitting, you need this book!! I loved it.

Kelly answers every question you ever thought of asking..........and dozens you never dreamed were relevant. I wish I'd had it 30 years ago when I began 'nomading.' Her insights, suggestions, and behind-the-scenes observations about the housesitting world (including a list of dozens of websites to search) will literally open doors all over the world."

— **Rita Golden Gelman**
Author, *Tales of a Female Nomad,*
Living at Large in the World

"KELLY HAS WRITTEN A LIVELY, upbeat and informative guide to introduce newcomers to the fascinating world of house sitting. The book is liberally scattered with insider tips, words of wisdom and amusing anecdotes from Kelly's own extensive experience."

— **Ian Usher & Vanessa Anderson**
Publishers, *House Sitting — The Ultimate Lifestyle Magazine*
www.HouseSittingMagazine.com
Founders, www.MapaHub.com — A connecting website exclusively for housesitters

"KELLY HAS NOT ONLY OFFERED great tips for anyone who wants to housesit, she's captured the spirit of housesitting in her humor and 'go-with-the-flow' attitude. I highly recommend this book!"

— **Donna Carvell**
Founder, *HouseSittingCafe Facebook group*

"ALTHOUGH I'VE NEVER HOUSESAT, I've been intrigued about it. *How to Become a Housesitter* has taught me how to successfully create a profile, land a sit and avoid pitfalls! This book is filled with specific information and tips gleaned from the author's years of personal experience. And, unlike other 'how to' books, this one is fun to read."

— **Ken Bridges**
Traveler and Future Housesitter

"MY HUSBAND AND I JUST COMPLETED our first sit, and the practical information Kelly shares in her book was invaluable! And her personal essays about her experiences are great fun to read."

— **Margaret Porter**
Daily newspaper publisher (retired)

"AFTER A YEAR OF FULLTIME housesits around the world with my husband, I felt we'd seen and done it all. Kelly's book made me realize we still have a lot left to learn. If we had read this book before we started traveling, I am sure we would have avoided a few unhappy mistakes and saved ourselves a bundle on travel expenses, too."

— **Tracy McDermott**
½ of the McNomads travel duo

"THE ADVICE AND TIPS Kelly generously offers in her book are spot on!"

— **Diane White Daniel**
Photographer, www.new-nomads.com
Fulltime digital nomad and housesitter

"THIS IS THE BOOK I WISH I'D HAD a few years ago when I first began my global housesitting adventures! Seasoned housesitters and homeowners are sure to gain many insights from these housesitting secrets. Infused with her vivacious personality, Kelly shares some of her intimate experiences making this book a fun and very enjoyable read."

— **Julie Bryant**
Founder and Creative Director
Naked Dragon Inspirational Events
www.nakeddragon.co.uk

"'WOW' AS IN 'BOW-WOW' (more information and tips than I thought I needed to know!). 'Perrrr....fect' (enjoyed reading Kelly's adventures)."

— **Aileen Landau**
Budget Travel Guru

"I WILL BE ABLE TO TRUST ANY HOUSESITTER who has read this detailed book — what to look out for, and how to make it a good experience for us both!"

— **Pauline Field**
Author
Feisty & Fearless: Nice Girls CAN Be Leaders
www.PaulineField.com

HOW TO BECOME A HOUSESITTER

INSIDER TIPS FROM THE HOUSESIT DIVA

KELLY HAYES-RAITT

Published by Living Large Press
http://www.BecomeAHousesitter.com

First Edition: June 2017

Cataloging – in –Publication Data

Hayes-Raitt, Kelly, author.

How to become a housesitter : insider tips from the

HouseSit diva / by Kelly Hayes-Raitt.

pages cm

ISBN 978-0-9989896-2-4

1. Housesitting--Handbooks, manuals, etc. 2. Pet sitting--Handbooks, manuals, etc. 3. Hayes-Raitt, Kelly --Anecdotes. 4. Handbooks and manuals. 5. Anecdotes.

I. Title.

TX321.H39 2017   640

QBI17-801

Dedicated to ChaCha and Charley, whose patience with me is boundless, and to all the dogs, cats and rabbits who welcomed me into their homes and allowed me to love them.

TABLE OF CONTENTS

Introduction   1

1. Can I Housesit with My Partner, Kids or   5
   Pets?
   Profiles of Actual Housesitters

2. Is Housesitting Right for Me?   9
   A Quiz: 30 Questions to Ask Yourself

3. Sounds Too Good to be True! What's the   17
   Downside?
   The Bitch & The Chow

4. To Charge or Not to Charge?   27

5. OK, I'm Ready! How Do I Start?   31
   25 Considerations...

6. OK, Now I'm REALLY Ready!   41
   How (and Where) Do I Build
   My Profile?
   Links to 50 Housesitting Platforms
   + A 20% Discount to Join the
   World's Largest Platform

7. Besides the Platforms, How Else Can I   55
    Find Housesits?
    11 Creative Ways to Find Housesits —
    for FREE

8. How Do I Know If a Sit Is Right for ME?   57
    1 Website Offers Practical Travel Info for
    230 Countries
    Keeping Abreast of the Language

9. How Do I Land My First Sit?   63
    8 Tips to a Better Application

10. I've Been Short-Listed! Now What?   67
    Checklist for the Skype Interview

11. Agreed, Now What?   71

12. Seriously? I Got the Sit! Now What?   73
    Puppy Love

13. OMG, What Have I Gotten Myself Into!   83
    8 Tips for Alleviating the Pre-Trip
    Heebie-Jeebies

14. OK, I'm Here! Now What?   87
    Checklist of 13 Things to Discuss
    with the Homeowners

15. Living on Top of Other People's Stuff   91
    14 Tips to Keeping Track of Your Stuff

16. Leaving A Great Impression   95
    7 Things to Consider

17. Getting Asked Back   99
    Between the Lines

18. When Things Go Wrong   105
    Not That Kind of Buzzed!"

19. Shhhh!   113
    3 Secret Tips to Landing Great Housesits

20. BONUS FOR HOMEOWNERS: 117
    How to Housesitter-Proof Your Home

21. ANOTHER BONUS FOR HOMEOWNERS: 119
    10 Ways Homeowners Can Welcome Their New Housesitter

22. A Final Note   121
    Stay In Touch!

Acknowledgements   123

About the Author   127

Coming Soon!   129

INTRODUCTION

OK, OK, I ADMIT IT: I sleep around.

Usually with animals.

(Being able to say that with a straight face is one of the reasons I continue housesitting.)

If you've ever dreamt of "living like a local" rather than being pegged as a tourist...

If you'd like to test what living in a community is like before committing to a permanent move...

If you want to save thousands of dollars on accommodations in some of the world's most glorious hotspots...

If you want to visit your grandkids or parents without being underfoot...

Or if you simply like sleeping around...

This book is for you! Gleaned from my real-world experiences during eight years of fulltime housesitting and pampering dozens of dogs, cats, bunnies and fish, this book contains advice and "insider tips" to help you leap into the world of housesitting with confidence and grace.

Whether you want to housesit fulltime as a lifestyle, or occasionally during your vacations, this book will help you avoid the pitfalls so many new housesitters (and seasoned ones, too) fall into.

You might wonder why I'm sharing my personal tips for securing great housesits. I believe traveling is transformative — not only for the traveler, but for all the people she or he meets along the way. Now more than ever, we need to open our hearts and homes to each other. Housesitting is one way to expand traveling opportunities, so I want to shout it out to the world!

If you are a homeowner with pets who has felt unable to travel because you refuse to kennel your "fur-kids," this book shows you how to find the most caring, conscientious housesitters. Two chapters at the end speak directly to homeowners! Personally, I wouldn't have strangers live in my home unless they've read this book.

I include *discount codes* for some of the more popular housesitting platforms (so the book pays for itself immediately!) and a quiz ("Is Housesitting Right For

Me?") so you can determine your own particular joys or challenges of housesitting.

To find where in the world I am now, visit me at www.BecomeAHousesitter.com. Or feel free to email me directly at Kelly@LivingLargeInLimbo.com.

Happy Housesitting!

Chapter 1

CAN I HOUSESIT WITH MY PARTNER, KIDS OR PETS?

MOST HOUSESITTERS DON'T housesit fulltime, as I do. They have homes they live in and housesit during their vacations, often finding housesitters for their own homes and pets. Others take a year off between jobs or other transitions and housesit during these periods. Still others housesit in a variety of locales as a way of trying out a new place to settle. Others housesit to be near grandchildren or ailing parents. Increasingly, there are housesitters who have sold off their homes and belongings and are fulltime modern nomads.

So, housesitters come in all varieties: Young digital nomads, retirees, families on vacation, people with their own pets in tow....And the great news is that there are housesits to fit every lifestyle!

Here are profiles of actual housesitters:

Julie, a single midlife freelancer, housesits most of the year between her gigs as an event planner, and has housesat in the U.K., Singapore, Mexico and the Middle East.

Tracy & Peter, a mid-career couple, took a year off during a transition to travel by housesitting. They've housesat in Thailand, Malaysia, Mexico, England, France, Australia, Sweden, and the U.S.

Randy & Gail, a retired American/Canadian couple, now housesit fulltime. They've cared for pets throughout North America and are "trying on" a community in Mexico as a potential permanent new base by housesitting.

Sheila & Kai are mid-40s digital nomads who have been housesitting in Mexico fulltime since 2013.

Nik & Dave, an American gay couple, housesit overseas during their vacations.

Dee, a freelance journalist in Canada, escapes winter by housesitting in Ajijic, Mexico, for two or three months over the holidays.

Melanie & Chris, an American couple, housesit during their vacations and secure housesitters to care for their fur-family at their home.

Carolyn housesits in her hometown a few times each year to be near her ailing father and to relieve her stepmother from fulltime caretaking.

Vanessa & Ian, modern digital nomads who publish *House Sitting Magazine* have housesat in the U.S., Australia, Fiji, U.K., Panama, Nicaragua, Botswana and Mexico since 2013.

Donna housesits fulltime with her husband and four-year-old daughter. Her experiences as a housesitting family inspired her to create a Facebook group, HouseSittingCafe.

Jodie, a 30-something Brit, housesat for me for three months in Los Angeles while exploring job opportunities for a fulltime move. She now produces a popular talk show.

Camille, an American living in Mexico, housesits with her Chihuahua while caring for others' pets, too. Since she lives within driving distance, she has the advantage of meeting homeowners before the sit to see how their pets interact.

Jennifer and John fly from London to Australia for a month every year and housesit to be near their grandchildren.

Diane and David are fulltime slow-travel nomads who have been house sitting in Mexico and Europe since 2009. He's a business consultant who can work on the road and she's an award-winning photographer.

Mark and Maria specialize in spoiling cats. They started housesitting in Australia and New Zealand, moved to SE Asia and are now based in Europe.

Del, a retired consultant in Phoenix whose husband is still working, gets her beach fix through regular Southern California housesits.

David, a 50-year-old Los Angeles lawyer and writer, visits me annually in Mexico (with permission from the homeowners, of course) and takes over my housesit so I can travel a bit. He's a substitute housesitter.

> 🐾 INSIDER TIP: Go for housesits where the homeowners mirror you. If you're housesitting with your kids, you are more likely to be chosen by a family. If you're housesitting by yourself, you are more likely to be chosen by a single homeowner. 🐾

Chapter 2

IS HOUSESITTING RIGHT FOR ME?

I DIDN'T WAKE UP one morning and declare, "I'm going to become a housesitter today!" It's a lifestyle that evolved following a career setback: After 30 years as a political activist/consultant, I'd run for office myself and gotten my butt kicked. I'd decided to take a sabbatical to write a book about my experiences in the Middle East working with refugees. (That book is still in progress...Check www.LivingLargeInLimbo.com for updates.)

To finance fulltime writing, I rented out my own home and, thus, needed to live elsewhere for free. Initially, I lived in writers' colonies where I'd been awarded residencies, but I gravitated to housesitting, which provided greater opportunities and was far less competitive. (At times, when my home is unrented, I've found housesitters, so I've experienced both sides of the housesitting coin.)

Since I couldn't live at my home, my first housesits were interspersed with writing residencies and visits with friends and family. My first year of "nomading" — 2009 — I drove across the U.S. four and a half times, slept in 58 beds and packed and unpacked 64 times. So, I've been sleeping around for a while.

2010 found me in Ajijic, Mexico, a large expat community south of Guadalajara. I fell into a dream sit: Six months every year spoiling ChaCha, a rambunctious pit/lab rescue puppy who lives in a four-story home built into the side of a hill. Every level of this vacation home has panoramic views of the serene Lake Chapala. The homeowners treat me like family, and I'm blessed to have a "home base" when they are stateside.

Since 2009, I've housesat in multiple homes in Mexico, the U.S., Europe, Asia and now have regular sits in London, Cardiff, Berlin and Hanoi. I've cared for bunnies from Copenhagen to Ya'an, China, a "village" of 1.5 million people where I met no other non-Asians during my entire 10-day sit. I've cuddled a 19-year-old Chihuahua in Kuala Lumpur and coaxed two feral cats in Osaka, Japan. For two months, I spoiled Merlin the mouser while enjoying London during the summer Olympics.

This year, I'll be caring for kitties in Amsterdam, Gibraltar, Senegal, Malawi and Mozambique.

Housesitting has turned out to be right for me. But, is it right for you?

The benefits of housesitting include the obvious cost savings in accommodations and dining (because you have a full kitchen at your fingertips), and the thrill of experiencing a destination as a local does.

But housesitting is not a free ride. Typically, you pay your own transportation, visa expenses and insurance. Most homeowners request that you arrive at least a day before their departure to orient you to the pets' and home's routines. If the homeowners do not have room to accommodate you on that first night, you might need to pay for a hotel.

There are a few other factors to housesitting that you might find challenging, such as adjusting your schedule to the homeowners', or living in their space on top of their belongings. Or you might find it stifling to be responsible for caring for someone else's home and pets and maintaining their rules, routines and schedules.

Some housesits include a household staff that is already in place: perhaps a housekeeper who might clean weekly, semi-weekly or daily, a gardener (or gardeners) who come weekly or semi-weekly, and/or a pool maintenance worker. It is the responsibility of the housesitter to "oversee" these workers in order to maintain the household's continuity. That can be a lovely luxury or a bothersome burden — depending on your perspective.

So, is housesitting a great opportunity for you? Here's a quiz to find out!

QUIZ:
IS HOUSESITTING RIGHT FOR ME?

INDICATE HOW STRONGLY you agree or disagree with the following statements on a scale of 1 to 5. Be honest! The last thing you want is to be miserable stuck in a commitment caring for a stranger's most prized pets and possessions.

Scale: 1 - Strongly Disagree   2 - Disagree
3 - Neutral   4 - Agree   5 - Strongly Agree

1. I feel at home wherever I am.

2. I get annoyed when I have to negotiate my schedule with other people's schedules.

3. When I am on vacation, I want to be taken care of and don't want to be responsible for anything.

4. I get anxious when I don't have my own space.

5. I love pets, even if they aren't mine.

6. I appreciate that the neighbors come by to say "hello." It makes me feel welcomed and a part of the neighborhood.

7. I just can't get comfortable when I'm not sleeping in my own bed.

8. When I am away from home, I love having a kitchen to make my morning coffee or tea.

9. I get annoyed when I can't figure out how to work the TV or if the cable stations aren't familiar to me.

10. Every home has its individual quirks; it's no big deal.

11. Clutter makes me anxious.

12. I don't trust other people to consider my needs when making their vacation plans.

13. Pets should follow my schedule and routines, regardless of the homeowners' instructions.

14. I get nervous having someone else's housekeeper in my space.

15. When I travel, I like to blend in like a local.

16. I don't trust people to keep their word.

17. It's disorienting living on top of other people's stuff.

18. When I travel, I want to be anonymous.

19. I love gardening — no matter where I am.

20. I resent having to email updates to virtual strangers about their house.

21. It's more authentic to live in a "real" neighborhood when I travel, rather than in a hotel.

22. I get frustrated when my kitchen doesn't have everything I want at my fingertips.

23. Wow, I'm so lucky to have this peaceful garden to enjoy my afternoon tea in....And it's "mine"!

24. It's annoying that the shower's water pressure is weak.

25. Pets enrich my life, and I enjoy shaking up my habits to keep them safe and happy.

26. When I am in others' homes, I'm nervous I might break something.

27. I need my own closet space.

28. It's fun to peruse other people's books.

29. I can make the bathroom space my own, regardless of how cluttered the medicine cabinet is.

30. I can find the "win/win" in almost every situation.

Give yourself 1 point for every "1," 2 points for every "2," etc. for questions 1, 5, 6, 8, 10, 15, 19, 21, 23, 25, 28, 29 and 30.

Give yourself 1 point for every "5," 2 points for every "4," 3 points for every "3," 4 points for every "2," and 5 points for every "1" for questions 2, 3, 4, 7, 9, 11, 12, 13, 14, 16, 17, 18, 20, 22, 24, 26 and 27.

131 — 150: You are a born housesitter! Consider housesitting as a lifestyle option.

91 — 130: Housesitting might be a great option for you to experience living like a local. Check the quiz again for those factors that make you most uncomfortable and be sure to raise them with the homeowners to minimize your discomfort. (For example, if your response to question #29 is "strongly disagree," then ask the homeowners if they would empty part of their medicine cabinet for you…or check out Chapter 15 for tips on keeping track of your stuff.)

30 - 90: Housesitting is just not for you. But there are other ways to experience living abroad that won't cause as much anxiety.

MOST IMPORTANT: Are you willing to forgo your sightseeing or vacation plans to care for the pet and home that have been left in your care when emergencies arise? If not, housesitting is not for you…

Read on for INSIDER TIPS to make housesitting your "new normal."

Chapter 3

SOUNDS TOO GOOD TO BE TRUE! WHAT'S THE DOWNSIDE?

HOMEOWNERS' SECOND WORST nightmare (after the fear of coming home to a trashed house and distraught pets) is that you won't show, leaving them stuck at the last minute with paid holiday plans and uncared-for pets.

Housesitters, on the other hand, have a plethora of nightmares. What if the house is a pigsty? Or unhealthy? What if the pets' routines are more complicated than the homeowners described? What if the pets escape, get sick...or worse? What if there's a natural disaster? Or a break-in? What if I break something? What if *I* have an emergency? What if the homeowners cancel or change plans at the last minute?

Believe it or not, during the eight years I've been a fulltime housesitter, most of those "what ifs" have happened to me.

Let's break it down and learn from my experiences:

→ What if the house is a pigsty or unhealthy for me?

A Skype tour of someone's home doesn't disclose filth or smells. The kitchen in a housesit in Japan was covered in sticky grime. I literally washed one plate, fork and glass for me to use during my stay and avoided using the kitchen as much as possible. Additionally, cicadas the size of my palm kept entering through the cat flap.

I had to keep reminding myself that this unusual sit gave me the freedom to leave overnight for a few days at a time so I could travel to Hiroshima and Nagasaki for the 70th commemorations of the atomic bombings. It was also conveniently located near a central metro station.

A sit in Malaysia was for a chain smoker whose home was delightfully decorated with myriad colorful curtains, which, regrettably, captured the smoky smell. It took a few days to air the place out. My sit in Ya'an was in an old Chinese apartment that was riddled with mold. I moved out of the bedroom and slept on the comfy sofabed.

Each of these sits was for less than two weeks. I figure I can put up with anything for just a couple of weeks. (And if I can't, then I don't take the sit.)

→ What if the pets' routines are more complicated than the homeowners described?

During a February housesit in Kent, England, the two adorable terriers woke me throughout the night to go out. They woke me at different times from each other, and at different times during the night, no matter how late I let them out before retiring. For six weeks, I didn't get more than four hours of sleep at a time. Luckily, I'm a writer who can handle irregular hours and nap during the day. When the homeowners returned, I asked them about this and they said they sleep with their backdoor open.

Now, I ask a lot of questions about pets' sleeping habits, their nighttime routines, what to do if they won't sleep, how to handle undesirable behavior, and hope the homeowners tell the truth. I laughingly mention this experience during our Skype interview so I can gauge the homeowners' reactions.

→ What if the pets escape, get sick...or worse?

Every housesitter's worst nightmare is having something happen to the pet. While I, very fortunately, have not had any pets die or run away on my watch, I do discuss that with the homeowners beforehand. (Do they want to be notified immediately, or wait until they return from their holiday?) I've dealt with a cat with colitis and a dog recovering from hip surgery. It's all part of the responsibility.

→ What if there's a natural disaster? Or a break-in?

Disasters, natural and man-made, are part of homeownership. As the stand-in homeowner, I prepare myself with phone numbers and instructions to deal with broken pipes or busted windows. I've housesat through an earthquake and I've had my laptop stolen by the household help. Preparation eases the stress.

→ What if I break something?

As careful as a housesitter is, it's almost inevitable that something will break. I ask homeowners to put away any special items that are valuable or sentimental. And we thoroughly go over instructions for using all appliances — particularly if I'm in a foreign country. If I break a glass or a dish, I ask the homeowners how I can replace it. One homeowner cheerfully told me she was planning on getting new dishes anyway, and I shouldn't worry about the dish I chipped.

→ What if I have an emergency?

I had just arrived at a six-week housesit in Hanoi when my father died back in Buffalo, NY. Although the homeowners had provided a backup sitter (something I always require) and totally supported my leaving, I decided to stay in Hanoi and Skype into the memorial service. One factor: I had only a single-entry visa to

Vietnam. Getting another visa would have taken at least a week. From now on, I'll be sure to pay for a multi-entry visa wherever I can to give me more flexibility.

I always ask for information about and directions to the nearest hospital, medical clinic and pharmacy in case I need medical care.

And I provide the homeowners with my own personal emergency contacts.

→ What if the homeowners cancel or change plans at the last minute?

During my first year of housesitting, a homeowner cancelled our agreement two days before my arrival, with no regard to leaving me stranded, as I was driving en route to her home after arranging my schedule around hers. (See *The Bitch & The Chow* after this chapter.) Fortunately, I had friends in the same city who took me in. Never put yourself in a position where you don't have a Plan B.

But the thing I find the most challenging is leaving animals I've bonded with. Fortunately, many of the homeowners for whom I've sat have invited me back.

❧ INSIDER TIP: Flexibility, resourcefulness, perspective, willingness to look on the bright side, and a sense of humor are a housesitter's best tools! ❧

THE BITCH AND THE CHOW

TO WRITE MY FIRST BOOK, I slept around by house- and petsitting rent-free, usually uneventfully. Until, that is, I nearly met Pixie, a chow-chow with separation anxiety so severe she once threw herself through a plate glass window.

However, Cheryl, Pixie's owner, assured me in her syrupy voice that Pixie had been through extensive therapy and was doing better. Good thing. She could not, however, be left alone for more than a quick grocery run. Figuring this housesit was only for a week while Cheryl and her husband cruised to Mexico, I decided to hermit with Pixie and start my book's next chapter. After all, while in residence at the girlhood home of American writer Carson McCullers in Columbus, Georgia, I hardly left the house, preferring to hunker down and write. Even while living in urbane Decatur, I spent many housebound days writing with Bebe, a sleek grey cat who lobbied for an author's credit by regularly sauntering across my keyboard before settling into my lap. I figured Pixie would be a blessing by forcing me to leave the house twice a day for walks.

Cheryl was flatteringly insistent that I accept this housesit in Albuquerque, and it nestled between two other housesits. Still, I hesitated until she offered me the phone number of a previous housesitter. But how would I gingerly ask this stranger if it's the dog who's neurotic, or the dog owner? Former housesitter spared me by jumping right in: "Don't get me wrong," he said. "Cheryl is a nice person; Pixie is great." The chasm between the lines echoed loudly.

Since I would be spending the week with the "great" dog and not the "nice" dog owner, I agreed to this housesit (where I'd neither be compensated for my time or travel expenses nor incur any living costs) and started arranging my travel schedule around Cheryl's. Then the emails started. First it was a website featuring photos of the chow, written in first-person from Pixie's perspective. (No offense, but Pixie needs to keep her day job.) Then an email titled "A Beautiful Day in NM" with a photo attached. I assumed it would be a glorious sunset or a dashing roadrunner. Instead, it was an indoor close-up of Cheryl and Pixie. I now had more photos of that chow than of my own mother.

And the questions. Cheryl wanted to know my height and was obsessed with my travel plans after I left her house. My height? Just how tall is this chow? Cheryl offered to have me spend the night with her and her husband after they returned home, so I could spend a "couple of hours debriefing" them. A couple of hours? Just how complicated is this house?

My next housesit was in Buffalo, arranged around Cheryl's schedule. Seems not many Albuquerqueans want to fly to Buffalo, so flights are limited. I found a flight that left ABQ four hours before Cheryl's flight landed. It was an ancillary bonus that I wouldn't have to spend the night with this controlling, obsessive woman.

Suspecting she'd want Pixie watched for those few hours, I emailed her before I purchased my plane ticket. That's when I learned the depth of the dog owner's separation anxiety. She called me. Her frantic, panicked tone made *me* want to jump through a plate glass window. She told me she had lined up a girlfriend who was charging her to sit in her living room and watch her dog for six hours. Stephanie would come an hour before I was to leave so I could "debrief" Stephanie. Cheryl then shifted the conversation to when we would "debrief."

"Well, we can't speak when you're in the air," she said in that breathy, saccharine voice. "Perhaps when you're between flights on your way to Buffalo?"

"How about the next morning?" I ventured.

"Oh, yes, well let's see. But then you'll be two hours ahead of us. Oh," I could hear her hands wringing, "oh, we'll just have to find a time."

Suddenly she got even more tense. "Oh, now I have to figure out when you and Stephanie can meet before we leave."

It wasn't a total surprise when Cheryl called me two days before my arrival to sing-song that I was "free" and didn't need to show up. Without a regard to my schedule, or anyone else's that had been arranged around hers, and without even an apology, Cheryl was downright gleeful that she was stranding me with this eleventh-hour cancellation.

After uttering a string of epithets that made everyone within earshot suspect I'd suddenly contracted Tourette's, I realized this was just another opportunity to find faith. I was being spared — or in Cheryl's words "freed" — to allow something better to enter my life. I just needed to trust. Well, I needed trust and a stiff drink. And chocolate.

But life worked out. The next day a friend offered an available bedroom in her Albuquerque house, free from anxious chows, controlling bitches and beckoning plate glass windows.

Chapter 4

TO CHARGE OR NOT TO CHARGE?

WHEN MOST PEOPLE HEAR that I housesit fulltime, they assume that I charge for my services. While some housesitters do charge for housesitting, I prefer to make my arrangement a quid pro quo: I get free accommodations in exchange for taking care of the home and pet, handling emergencies and communicating regularly with the homeowners. I prefer to be treated as a responsible houseguest than as a household employee….but that's a very personal choice.

I pay for my own travel to the sitting assignment, so I prefer sits that are longer or can be combined with others to make my travel costs worthwhile. Every once in a while, homeowners who live in a more remote location will offer to contribute to my travel costs, realizing that they are saving a bundle on pet boarding costs.

Many housesitters who get paid for caring for pets live locally and don't have the benefit of exploring a new area. These housesitters develop ongoing relationships with the pets they care for and are often available for frequent short assignments. Some homeowners prefer this type of relationship because it provides more continuity for their pets, particularly if they travel for just two or three days at a time or if their pets have special needs.

Some housesitters charge for duties that might be considered beyond the ordinary: Caring for a pet that needs surgery, for example, or staying in a home that is undergoing remodeling.

Then, there's the dynamic of the homeowners asking the housesitter to pay for or take on unpaid duties beyond normal petsitting and trouble-shooting, such as:

Managing bed & breakfasts, vacation rentals or AirBnB guests where the responsibilities include cleaning the units, greeting guests and trouble-shooting.

"Looking in on" an elderly parent, managing a tenant or interacting with an adult child living in the house.

Paying for utility costs. The homeowners might have been burned by previous housesitters who ran up large utility bills for a/c in the summer months or heat in the winter months. Personally, I refuse to pay for utilities, as I am quite conservative when it comes to using a/c or heat. I ask the homeowners about their usage that keeps them — and their pets — comfortable during the season I'll be housesitting, and I stay consistent.

Paying for their housekeeper. Although I have occasionally paid a housekeeper to continue during my assignment, I ask the homeowners to cover that cost. They benefit by having continuity, by knowing a trusted set of eyes is checking their house and by returning to a home cleaned exactly the way they like.

Every situation is unique. Clear communication and knowing your limits are so important!

🐾 INSIDER TIP: It's important to remember that if money does exchange hands, there might be tax implications for both you and the homeowners. Also, a paid gig might change the type of visa you need to enter the country from a tourist to a work visa. 🐾

Chapter 5

OK, I'M READY!
HOW DO I START?

THINK ABOUT THE TYPE of housesit you'd really like. Your needs will change, but here are some considerations:

Your Purpose for Housesitting

Is this a vacation for you? A working retreat? Are you a walkabout addict? Or are you filling in a gap between other housesits?

Thinking about what type of experience you'd like to have will eliminate a lot of housesits that wouldn't fill your needs — or your soul. For example, if you're looking for a cultural experience filled with museums, ballets and fine dining, a rural housesit won't likely be appropriate. On the other hand, if you are looking for a writing retreat, that farmhouse might be perfect!

Length

You might have only two weeks of holiday time, or you might be looking for a longer sitting assignment to "anchor" a multi-month trip. Or you might want a weekend to fill in before your flight home.

Your ideal housesit length will be determined not only by your travel logistics, but by your personal comfort level. Ask yourself: How often are you comfortable moving around — packing and unpacking? Are you a 28-cities-in-30-days type of traveler? Or a land-and-lump type? No single answer is correct and it will vary according to other circumstances, but it's part of the equation.

Country/Continent

Depending on how much time you have, you can choose a part of the world and build a series of housesits in that area. Choosing one area allows you to focus your sitting options and reduce airfares. For example, one summer, I chose a three-week housesit in Malaysia and then filled in two other Malaysia sits at either end.

During one two-month period, I took three assignments in Europe that were arranged around a repeat sit in Berlin: Berlin for 10 days, Amsterdam for a week, and Gibraltar for two weeks.

Time Zone

If you are telecommuting with your home office, the foreign time zone you housesit in might wreak havoc with your sleep cycles...and might not be worth it. Similarly, if you need to communicate with ill or elderly relatives back home, the time zone you housesit in should dovetail with those needs.

Rural/Urban

Are you a city or a country person? Do you want to be in the middle of town or in the middle of nowhere? Are you looking for stimulation or serenity?

Season

Will you be housesitting in the Caribbean during hurricane season? Up north in the winter? Consider whether you are prepared to handle a weather emergency.

Fitness Required

Is there an elevator to that seventh-floor flat? How energetic are the dog walks? Will you be at a high altitude?

Proximity to Grocery Stores, Etc.

Remember that you will need to handle everyday tasks. How easy will that be? This is more than just a lifestyle question. Do you want to drive in the foreign country you've chosen? If so, be sure to check insurance and international drivers license requirements. If not, be sure to determine how close you'll be to public transportation, grocery stores and restaurants. Is the walk home from the grocery store up a steep hill?

Garden/Pool/Hot Tub Maintenance Requirements

Are you prepared to take on these maintenance responsibilities?

Type of Pets

Horses? Iguanas? Rats? Snakes? Llamas? Birds? Rabbits? Donkeys? Be sure to know all the animals' requirements before accepting the sitting assignment. Know your limits!

Pets' Routines and Habits

Do the dogs need walking every four hours? That might be a drag for daylong sightseeing or it might be a blessing by forcing you away from your computer regularly.

What are the animals' sleeping habits? Do they sleep in the bed with you? Do they sleep through the night? What are their toilet habits?

Number of Pets

Eight cats? Three big dogs? Again, know your limits!

Pets' Needs

Do the pets need daily shots? Medication? Regular brushing? Again, be honest with yourself about your limits.

Bugs

Are you particularly allergic to fleabites? Wigged out by cockroaches? You might ask the homeowners about their flea control regimes (which you'd be required to maintain) and the bugs they deal with (and how those bugs are dealt with). If there are monthly exterminations scheduled, for example, and you are sensitive to chemicals, you might want to pass.

Nearby Noise

If silence is important to you, ask about nearby construction, barking dogs, street vendors' loud-speakers, partying neighbors, and church bells.

Will you be in the country during a political campaign exposing you to hourly loudspeaker announcements or during Ramadan's dawn and dusk calls to prayer?

Mold/Smoke

If you are allergic to mold or smoke, ask your homeowners about this beforehand. The last thing you want is to arrive at a destination and learn you can't breathe in the home.

House Clutter

Carefully look at the posted house photos and at the background during your Skype conversation to determine if the house's clutter and colors will work for you. It's challenging to clean thoroughly around excessive clutter, so take into account your need for white-glove clean corners.

Culture Shock

This is a very personal response to living in an area that is unlike your home culture. One of the joys of housesitting is living in a neighborhood as locals would. But this experience isn't for everyone. Be honest with yourself.

Isolation

Consider language, cultural and community barriers to connecting with locals. At a housesit I accepted in Ya'an, China, I was the only non-Asian person I encountered in ten days and had no face-to-face English conversation during that time. (Thank goodness for Skype!)

Ability to Speak Local Language

See above. Additionally, how will you communicate with any household staff?

Communication with Homeowners

Some homeowners want daily communication, others weekly or none at all. If a homeowner requires daily photos and/or texts, can you comply?

Oversight from Neighbors

Some homeowners ask their neighbors or relatives to drop by unannounced. Are comfortable with that?

Weather

Those photos on the housesit posting of the lush gardens and trees may not be representative of the weather during time of year of the housesit. Be sure to ask about heating (or cooling) systems and costs. Usually, the homeowners pay these utilities, but some homeowners have been stuck with large bills, so be sure to ask how you can be consistent with their usage.

Security

You might consider both the security of the location (including factors such as crime, terrorism, disease outbreaks and political stability) and of the home itself (alarm systems, nanny-cams, etc.).

Your Expenses

Be sure to factor in the cost of travel to the housesit at that time of year, visa expenses and the general cost of living at the location. Will you need to rent a car? Additionally, assume you will have unexpected expenses for items (such as a coffeemaker) that enhance your life.

Visa Requirements

Especially if you are considering a last-minute sitting assignment, the time involved in securing a visa might be a factor to consider.

Shots Needed

Consider your entire itinerary when researching required inoculations. You might not, for example, need a yellow fever shot to enter a country if you are coming from your home, but it might be required if you are visiting another country in the interim — even if you never leave the airport in the connecting country. Also pay attention to when you need to start taking the medication. You might need to start taking some meds (such as some malaria prophylaxis) two weeks before entering the country.

Access to Health and Emergency Services at Location

If you have personal health concerns, be sure to research options for your own health care. How far is the nearest clinic or emergency room? What types of services are offered and how are they paid for?

Internet Bandwidth and Reliability

If you are a digital nomad (or just a Skype addict), consider your specific needs for Internet reliability, bandwidth and download and upload speeds.

Other Responsibilities

You might not be comfortable running the home-owners' bed & breakfast or caring for their AirBnB guests in their absence. Or living with their adult child, elderly parent, roommates or renters.

You might have other considerations. For example, I once turned down a two-month housesit in London because there was no shower and I'd have to wash my hair in the kitchen sink. That would probably not be a deal-breaker for others, but it was for me. (The Skype tour of the home revealed that to me.)

> 🐾 INSIDER TIP: If you are traveling with a partner, be sure to review these considerations with him or her, so you can both be happy housesitters! 🐾

Chapter 6

OK, NOW I'M *REALLY* READY! HOW (AND WHERE) DO I BUILD MY PROFILE?

WHEN CREATING YOUR online profile, whether it's on a housesitting platform* such as Trusted House-sitters or Nomador, or on your own personal website, remember you are creating an online résumé. You may be competing against dozens of other applicants. (When I first listed my home in Santa Monica, CA, for a two-month sitting assignment, I had 80 applicants within 18 hours!) So, spending time creating an outstanding profile will be well worth your effort.

(*By "platform," I mean a particular housesitting website that allows you to purchase a membership, post a description of yourself, receive and send emails to other platform members and post and receive reviews of your housesitting experiences.)

There are four elements to your profile:

• The description that usually answers a couple of standard questions, such as "Why I want to housesit."

• Photos

• Video

• Reviews

Description

Create an engaging description of yourself that answers the question, "Why I want to housesit for YOU!" Show what you can bring to the "table." Don't just focus on what you get out of housesitting. Remember, you are providing a valuable service, not looking for free vacation digs.

Obviously, emphasize your experiences with pets and animals.

Include your experiences with managing or owning homes, pools, farms, bed & breakfasts.

Include any medical or veterinarian background.

Stand out by showing your personality. It's OK to take a risk and be controversial. In my profiles on Trusted Housesitters and Nomador, I mention that I'm writing a book about my experiences in the Middle

East with Iraqi refugees. That might turn off some people (and it has), but it has also floated me to the top of some very big lists.

Photos

Choose photos of yourself interacting with pets. You'd be surprised at the number of housesitter profiles that feature what appear to be police mug shots. Or, worse, people downing shots!

If including photos taken during previous house-sitting assignments, be sure they don't include any images that might compromise homeowners' security or privacy.

Video

Shoot a creative video. Peruse some of the profiles on the existing platforms and notice how boring many of the videos are. They're usually the sitter(s) sitting on a couch saying the same things that are written in the profile. We call those "talking heads." In writers' parlance, we say those videos "tell," not "show."

Don't just tell me you're responsible and flexible, SHOW your humor, your flexibility. Be someone the homeowners want to meet.

Again, be sure to protect the privacy and security of homeowners for whom you have housesat in the past.

Consider telling a story — perhaps the story of how you got into housesitting, or anecdotes of your personal interactions with pets.

Since I had run for public office, I decided to create a video that looks like a campaign commercial. It's silly, narrated by a friend of mine who pretended to be ChaCha, the rambunctious pit/lab rescue I care for every year in Mexico. But it's fun and says a lot about me in a very short time:

https://www.youtube.com/watch?v=LnyPrElP1_A

Reviews

Gather reviews as quickly following the sitting assignment as you can, while the homeowners are still feeling warm and glowy. Some platforms allow you to contact the homeowners through the platform, others will automatically send the homeowners a request for a review.

If the platform offers you a chance to respond to the review, do so, using the opportunity to provide even more information about yourself and your housesitting experience.

In response to one great review I received, I responded:

Sometimes, there are experiences that are just game-changers, and this housesit was one of them. I had already

*appreciated Jenny & Chris' clear communication and wel-
coming attitude before I arrived in Hanoi. What I wasn't
prepared for was this: Four days after I arrived, my Dad
died. Jenny & Chris were so caring, supportive and flexible
and offered back-up coverage for me if I decided to return to
the States.*

*In the end, for a variety of reasons, including — selfishly
— that I felt so loved by Brody I couldn't imagine leaving
him, I decided to stay. During our first two weeks together, I
have to confess, Brody took more care of me than me of him.
(How do animals know to do this?)*

*Yes, Brody was truly loved...And I felt, and feel, truly
loved by him, Jenny and Chris. I'm so honored they chose me
as their housesitter this summer, and I would relish the
opportunity to return! I feel I've made a new family in
Hanoi. Thank you, Brody, Jenny & Chris!*

In this response, I'm showing future homeowners
that I'm willing to stay, even through a personal emergency. Remember that responses are addressed to that
current homeowner, but are really for the benefit
of homeowners of FUTURE sitting assignments.

Finally

Some sitters prefer to create their profiles on their
own websites. While there are advantages to this (such
as collecting all reviews in one place), I prefer to build
my presence on one platform. I have several reasons
for this strategy:

Most of the platforms distinguish between reviews by homeowners who are also members of the platform ("internal" reviews) from "external" reviews. Since outside reviews can be faked, I, when interviewing potential sitters for my home in Santa Monica, lean toward applicants with "internal" reviews.

Homeowners looking for sitters can find me and approach me. Even if that particular sit won't work for me, this gives me the opportunity to start a relationship for a future sitting assignment.

Some homeowners won't visit a separate website.

> 🐾 INSIDER TIP: If you build a profile on Trusted Housesitters, the world's largest housesit site, use this code for a 20% discount www.TrustedHousesitters.com/su /yeQdSjaK — worth $23 US! 🐾

> 🐾HOT! INSIDER TIP: Apply to **three housesitting assignments for FREE** through the "Discovery Option" on www.Nomador.com, the world's only bilingual plat-form. 🐾

❧ HOT! INSIDER TIP for VEGETARIANS and VEGANS: www.KindredSpiritsHouse.com is currently offering FREE member-ships! ❧

❧ INSIDER TIP: Members of www.Nomador.com can "stop over" for a few nights and enjoy local hospitaltity! ❧

PLATFORMS

PLEASE NOTE: New platforms pop up all the time. Some of these are struggling and might be gone by press time. The first four listed have been around a while and have a variety of listings. Beyond that, you might want to follow a platform — particularly the regional/country ones — for a couple of months to see whether it's growing before joining it. And some of these sites are for paid sitters.

- www.TrustedHouseSitters.com

- www.MindMyHouse.com

- www.Nomador.com

- www.HouseSitMatch.com

- www.LuxuryHouseSitting.com

- www.TheHouseSittersNetwork.com

- www.KindredSpiritsHouse.com
  (for vegetarians and vegans)

- www.KingdomHouseSitters.com
  (for Christians)

Australia only:

- www.MindAHome.com.au

- www.HappyHouseSitters.com.au

- www.AussieHouseSitters.com.au

- www.AustralianHouseSitter.com.au

- www.HouseSittersAustralia.com.au

- www.EasyHouseSitting.com

- www.HouseSitting.world

- www.YourHomeMyHome.com.au

- www.HouseSittingTasmania.com.au

- www.FreeRangeCamping.com.au
  (for RVers)

- www.au.holidog.com
  (paid sitters)

- www.at.holidog.com
  (paid sitters)

- www.Tiersitter24.at
  (paid sitters)

Belgium only:

- www.be.holidog.com
  (paid sitters)

Brazil only:

- www.br.holidog.com
  (paid sitters)

Canada only:

- www.HouseSittersCanada.com

- www.HouseSitCanada.com

- www.HouseSitter.com
  (paid sitters)

France only:

- www.fr.holidog.com
  (paid sitters)

- www.ilidor.com
  (French language)

Germany only:

- www.de.holidog.com
  (paid sitters)

Italy only:

- www.it.holidog.com
  (paid sitters)

Mexico only:

- www.HouseSitMexico.com

Netherlands only:

- www.nl.holidog.com
  (paid sitters)

New Zealand only:

- www.HouseSitters.co.nz

- www.KiwiHouseSitters.co.nz

- www.TownAndCountryHomeSit.co.nz
  (Christchurch only)

- www.HomeSit.co.nz
  (paid sitters)

- www.nz.holidog.com
  (paid sitters)

Spain only:

- www.es.holidog.com
  (paid sitters)

Switzerland only:

- www.ch.holidog.com
  (paid sitters)

- www.Petsitting24.ch
  (paid sitters)

United Kingdom only:

- www.MindAHome.co.uk

- www.HouseSittersUK.co.uk

- www.HomeSitters.co.uk
  (paid sitters)

- www.uk.holidog.com
  (paid sitters)

- www.CatInAFlat.com
  (paid sitters)

- www.CatSittingNow.co.uk
  (paid sitters)

United States only:

- www.HouseSittersAmerica.com

- www.us.holidog.com
  (paid sitters)

- www.Rover.com
  (paid sitters)

- www.HouseSitter.com
  (paid sitters)

🐾 INSIDER TIP: To check available housesitting assignments on multiple sites at once, try www.HouseSitSearch.com.

This new powerful search engine is like www.kayak.com for housesitters, allowing you to type in filters such as specific dates, geographic regions, or the types of pets you prefer and will then scour many of the housesitting sites for assignments tailored to your needs. 🐾

Chapter 7

BESIDES THE PLATFORMS, HOW ELSE CAN I FIND HOUSESITS?

I'VE LANDED MOST of my housesits from www.TrustedHousesitters.com, but I've also reached homeowners through some creative outreach, including:

Posting on housesitting groups on Facebook, such as HouseSittingCafe. I'm an active member, so when someone posted looking for a sitter for a friend in Langkawi, I was tagged since the group knew I was already in Malaysia. I responded and landed the sit.

Posting on expat forums, such as www.Internations.org. That's how I landed a sit in Osaka.

Posting on location-specific expat Facebook groups.

Handing out housesitting business cards on planes and at the dog park.

Meeting pet-owning neighbors during housesits. This a great strategy for returning to areas you love.

Contacting local universities to find professors taking sabbaticals.

Contacting universities and schools that hire expats as teachers. As expats often travel during their breaks, this is a great strategy for getting longer summer and holiday sits.

Contacting English-language magazines that are read by expats. You might offer to write an article about housesitting — mentioning, of course, your desire for a future sit.

Posting on local websites that publicize free stuff and services, such as www.NextDoor.com.

Posting notices on bulletin boards where expats hang out (expat societies, coffee shops, etc.). Expats offer great housesits, as they often travel for longer periods.

Contacting veterinarians in communities where you hope to sit.

...And, of course, spreading word-of-mouth among your peeps!

Chapter 8

HOW DO I KNOW IF A SIT IS RIGHT FOR ME?

BEFORE APPLYING FOR a sitting assignment, go back and check the considerations listed in Chapter 5. Choose the top three considerations that are important to you in your next sit and apply only for sits that meet those needs. Don't allow yourself to be seduced by sits that sound sexy, but in reality would be a terrible fit for you. Everyone loves his or her own home, but that doesn't mean you will.

Check the homeowners' posting carefully. How thorough is it? Does it look as if the homeowners spent some time preparing it? If not, that's not necessarily a deal-breaker, but it is an indication they probably won't spend a lot of time interviewing housesitters.

Does the description include information that would make a housesitter comfortable — or is it all about the pets and their needs? Again, that's not a deal-breaker, but it's an indication of the homeowners' priorities.

Do the photos show the home — or are they only of the pets?

Some of the platforms indicate who the past sitters are. Is this the homeowners' first experience with a sitter? I've done several sits for first-time homeowners, and I spend more time with them asking questions.

If past sitters are listed, click on their profiles so you can see the type of sitter the homeowners like. Did the homeowners leave a review? What did they mention in the review that they appreciated?

Are there housesitters that have repeated for these homeowners? That's a great indication that the homeowners know how to form and nurture relationships.

Consider whether this sit will require you to have a car. Will the homeowners allow you to use theirs? What are the costs of insurance? Will your driver's license be legal?

Check your health insurance policy. Will it cover you in this location? If not, what other health care options to you have?

Think about the cultural and language differences not only in the location, but also with the homeowners themselves.

Consider your ability to stay connected. Does your cellphone plan work in this country? Can you easily post to Facebook and other social media sites? (While in Ya'an, China, where Facebook is illegal, I connected through a VPN that my homeowner hosts provided for me.)

While housesitting in Africa, nearly every account I have either required extra verification or blocked me completely because I was logging on from Africa. I wish I had arranged a VPN subscription beforehand!

Check your government's foreign travel website for up-to-date safety and security advisories. You might wish to sign up for warnings issued to travelers by the U.S. State Department. (You do not need to be an American citizen.)

Factor in opportunities to travel and sightsee before or after the sitting assignment.

Research the location — cost to travel there, cost of visas, vaccination requirements. A great site that lists all the travel info you need in one place — weather, currency, relative price of things, ATMs, visa requirements, emergency numbers, location of your embassy, type of electrical sockets, tipping etiquette, etc. — is www.TheBaseTrip.com.

Research the cost of living by checking out www.Numbeo.com, which provides city-to-city cost comparisons.

🐾 INSIDER TIP: While your interaction with the pets is obviously important, your most important relationship is with the homeowners, even if you spend very little time with them. 🐾

KEEPING ABREAST OF THE LANGUAGE

NOT ALL FOREIGN HOUSESITS are created equal. I have a recurring housesit in Ajijic, Mexico, one of the world's largest expatriate communities. The community has been quite "gringo-ized": I grocery shop at Wal-Mart.

During one shopping trip, I approached the deli counter to buy chicken breasts, but I didn't know the Spanish verbiage.

"Quiero seis pollo de este," I blurted while pointing quickly at my own breast. ("I'd like six chicken, uh....")

Without missing a beat, the Mexican guy behind the counter responded in perfect English, "We don't have any that big."

For the record, the word for "chicken breast" is *pechuga*.

Chapter 9

HOW DO I LAND MY FIRST SIT?

AFTER YOU CREATE and post a fabulous profile, join a couple of Facebook groups and let your tribe know about your desire to housesit, you can land that first sit by following these tips:

Go local first. It's easier to network in your own community where you'll be available to meet homeowners in person as they choose their next housesitter. Also, by being local, they can rest assured you'll show up on time. Be sure to ask for a review on your profile, even if you secured the sit from a source other than the platform where your profile is posted.

Make yourself available during the busiest vacation times: Christmas, Chinese New Year (for SE Asia sitting assignments), summers.

Join the smaller, country-specific platforms where there is likely to be less competition than on the larger platforms.

Write a great application letter! This is your first contact with the homeowners and it needs to be outstanding. Remember, you are competing against several other (perhaps several dozen other) house-sitters to care for someone's home and beloved pets.

To write an exceptional letter, follow these tips:

Address the homeowners by name.

Mention the pets by name.

Respond to specific requests the homeowners mentioned in their posting (e.g., your ability to handle large dogs or your willingness to administer medication).

Elaborate on what you have to offer the homeowners (e.g., your experience with maintaining pools or your ability to garden).

Mention why you'd like to visit their community. Show some enthusiasm for their country or city.

Be personal. Just as in your profile, the more you can show your personality, the more likely you will grab attention.

Offer an alternative way to reach you and a next step, which could be answering their questions or Skyping.

🐾 INSIDER TIP: In your application letter, indicate that you've researched visa requirements and flight costs and that these don't pose a problem. This shows you are not responding to every housesit, but that you've spent a bit of time researching their specific location. 🐾

Chapter 10

I'VE BEEN SHORT-LISTED!
NOW WHAT?

ONCE YOU'VE BEEN "short-listed," request a Skype interview. This interview should be non-negotiable. This is an opportunity for the homeowners to interview you, but it's also an opportunity for you to interview them. If they don't, can't or won't Skype, ask yourself "why?" Is their Internet service lousy? Are they embarrassed about their home? Or are they hiding something? Not being willing to Skype to meet the person who might care for their pets and home should raise a red flag.

During the call, ask for a visual tour of the home. Look for clutter, ashtrays, light, and the considerations from Chapter 5 that are important to you. Ask about the three things you identified that are most important to you (noise? smoke? location?).

Here are questions you might include in your conversation, and be sure to ask about your top three deal-breakers:

About the Pet(s)

What are Fido's favorite things?

Where does he sleep? What are his nighttime habits? Does he sleep through the night?

How does he misbehave? How do you handle it?

What is your flea control regime?

Do you have a trusted friend I can call if there's a problem?

About the Home

Ask about things that are important to you: Internet speed, kitchen appliances, shower/bathtub, cable package, bugs, noise?

Are there any issues with neighbors?

About the Neighborhood/Community

Ask about things that are important to you about the location: Nearest grocery store, public transportation?

What is the cost of living like?

Any recent break-ins or robberies?

About Living in Third World Countries

What do you do for drinking water?

How often does the electricity go out?

How reliable is the Internet?

About Them

How do you like to be communicated with? How often?

Have you had housesitters before? How did it go? What worked? What didn't?

Ask this difficult question: What if the unthinkable happens with your pet? Some homeowners want to know immediately, others want to wait until they come home. What would you prefer?

If your call is going well and the sitting assignment will work for you, try to close the deal. Say: "I'm excited! What additional information can I give you? I'd love to care for Fido and your home!"

If they offer you the sitting assignment, let them know that you have an agreement you'd like to email them. (That's Chapter 11.)

Finally, ask yourself: "If this sit is not as described (if the house is messy, the pets are more work than described), can I deal with it? Am I willing to take this chance to be in an area I want to explore, or to be settled between sits, or to use this as a jumping-off point for other sits in the region, or to get initial experience?"

Be honest with yourself. If the answer is "no," move along. Resist the temptation to "talk yourself into" a sitting assignment because you are afraid of a currently empty space in your calendar. The last thing you want is to be committed to an experience that is not right for you. There are plenty of other sits in the sea!

🐾 INSIDER TIP: Listen to your gut. Now that you've gathered information, pay attention to your intuition. Both are valuable. 🐾

Chapter 11

AGREED, NOW WHAT?

A WRITTEN AGREEMENT is an important ingredient, but a controversial one. I firmly believe in having homeowners (particularly those who have never had a housesitter) fill out my housesitter agreement. I make exceptions for homeowners who have had multiple housesitters and have created their own house manual. I still require them to email me their specific travel plans (so that I have it in writing) and I cross-check my agreement with their house manual because my agreement is often more thorough.

(Other housesitters say we should rely just on our instinct. While instinct is important, a written agreement records the most basic info: travel dates, emergency contacts. It's a document that you can refer back to.)

I also offer my agreement to homeowners to use with other housesitters. It's a comprehensive questionnaire to put all of the homeowners' info in one place. I offer it to you. Feel free to adapt it to your use and your needs (review Chapter 5).

🐾 INSIDER TIP: To get a FREE download of the agreement I use, please visit http://bit.ly/2pikmKz. Revise it to reflect the things that are most important to you. 🐾

Chapter 12

SERIOUSLY?
I GOT THE SIT! NOW WHAT?

CONGRATULATIONS! You've landed the sit, created a great relationship with the homeowners and done your homework about how to get there. Now what?

Research your cellphone service. Do you have unlimited texting from the country where you'll be living? This is important because it will determine how you communicate with the homeowners — and with your own peeps.

Buy your ticket by cloaking your travel searches and limiting "cookies." Conduct private browsing by hitting Shift + Command + N (Safari) or Shift + Command + P (Firefox), or go to "file → new private window."

This will allow you to conduct searches on www.kayak.com, www.momondo.com, and www.skyscanner.com for the best tickets without your browsing history affecting the price.

Get creative with your ticket searches. Sometimes the cheapest ticket isn't from Point A to Point B. For a housesit in Berlin, for example, I flew from Los Angeles (my home base) to Oslo on Norwegian Air for $138 US. That gave me an overnight in Oslo, a city I'd never visited, with a separate ticket to Berlin the next day, saving me $273 US.

To get to a housesit in Hanoi from Los Angeles one summer, one-way tickets were $800+. But I found a one-way ticket from Vancouver, Canada, which has a large Vietnamese population, to Guangzhou, China, for less than half that. The savings allowed me to visit friends in Seattle, have a three-night layover in Guangzhou to explore (and to get over my jetlag, so I arrived at my housesit fresh), fly easily to Hanoi, and still save $200 US!

Look for new routes with specials and regularly discounted routes to find alternative, cheaper routing. Be sure to check visa requirements and procedures for any country where you intend to lay over.

There are dozens of search sites out there, but I use Kayak Explore and www.SecretFlying.com to check out airfares to the region where I'll be housesitting — not to the specific destination. That's how I pieced together the Guangzhou ticket I describe above.

Additionally, Kayak's "flex date" searches may reveal cheaper tickets a day or two earlier — sometimes the flight savings covers more than a hotel in a coveted destination.

Get your visa ahead of time, if possible. Especially if you will be in the country for a while, pay extra for a multi-entry visa. As previously mentioned, I had just arrived in Hanoi for a six-week sit when my father in Buffalo, NY, died. One of the factors that made it difficult for me to go back for his memorial service was that my visa — which had been a real pain to get — was single-entry, and I'd have to go through the entire visa application process again, delaying my return to my committed housesit. (I Skyped into the memorial service.)

Connect via cellphone (What's App, text messaging) with the homeowners before you travel, so you are certain you have the correct information if you need to reach them once you arrive in their city.

Text the homeowners again when you arrive to be sure your phones are connected. This tests how your phone works in their country. Once the homeowners leave, if there's a connecting issue it's more likely in the country they are visiting.

As you go through Customs, do not say you are housesitting. Many countries consider this "work," even though you are not paid, and require a different type of visa. By now, you are truthfully a tourist visiting friends!

Some countries are touchier to enter. Be ready with printed itineraries, travel e-tickets, or other documentation to show you will be leaving the country. At some Custom desks, they will not allow you to turn on your cellphone or access the Internet, so printed documentation is important.

If the country you are entering requires an ongoing ticket confirming your departure, and you are not ready to purchase one, you can "rent" a one-way ticket through several sites such as www.NomadProof.ca, www.FlyOnward.com, or www.BestOnwardTicket.com. For a small fee (usually less than $20 US), these firms will purchase a one-way ticket in your name from the country you are entering to another destination — a ticket you will not use but will meet the Custom's requirement.

Pre-check Skype or other long-distance Internet service from the country where you'll be living — and from the home itself. When I was in Ya'an, China, for example, I needed to access Skype through a VPN account (which the homeowners generously provided).

When researching your travel arrangements, look for layover programs. Often, as a way to promote tourism, a country's airline partners with their local tourism bureau to offer incredible layover bargains. For example, the cheapest flight between housesits in Japan and the U.K. one summer was on Emirates with an unusually long layover in Abu Dhabi. After researching, I found Emirates' stopover program. For about $150 US, I had two nights in a plush hotel, including breakfasts, and a chance to explore a new city and adjust to the new time zone.

A flight that cost less than half of competitors' between housesits in China and the U.K. was on Air Astana with a 23-hour layover in Almaty. (I had to go running for my atlas to find that one!) Almaty is the old capital city of Kazakhstan, so I took advantage of Air Astana's layover program: $90 US bought me a night in a hotel in the city's charming center, breakfast and airport transfers.

Find these deals by scouring both the airline's and the airport's websites. Be sure to check visa requirements. (Usually, a two- or three-day visa is included.) An unusually long layover is a tipoff that a promotional stopover program may exist.

PUPPY LOVE

I KNOW THE MOMENT I fell in love with Marcus. I was housesitting in Kent and caring for two terriers. On an early date, I suggested we take the pups for a long walk through the winding country roads in "my" neighborhood. Secretly, it was a test: How canine-compatible were we?

We were so engrossed in our conversation, we walked farther than intended. The younger terrier was in heaven, exploring off-lead and getting a great work-out. The older girl, however, was lagging and getting weary. Before I knew it, Marcus had scooped up all fifteen pounds of her wriggling weight and tucked her muddy little body into his coat. He carried her the whole way home! That was it: I was a smitten kitten.

Our relationship bloomed through each succeeding housesit. Since I live in Los Angeles and housesit in Mexico six months/year while I rent out my house, and he lives in London caring for his mum while he rents out his home in rural Wales, housesitting provided us the opportunity to be in the same postal code.

First, we housesat together for two weeks in Cardiff for two lively whippets. We explored the docks, the canals and our lives during our marathon dog walks and chats. Next, we spent a month together in Twickenham, a stone's throw from the Thames, where Marcus charmed a feisty calico — and me. We dined in riverside restaurants, played Scrabble in the local pub and competed over whose lap the cat would choose while we cuddled on the couch watching movies.

That fall, he flew to Mexico to join me in my recurring housesit for ChaCha, the rambunctious, smart pit/lab rescue I care for every spring and fall. Within moments, he had ChaCha eating out of his hand — both literally and figuratively. She reveled in the double-dose of playmates and I reveled in sharing the stunning views of Lake Chapala with my new British beau.

I just returned from a quick trip to the U.K. for his daughter's wedding and spent an extra week house-sitting in Sussex where Marcus joined me every night after work. We romped in London and revisited Richmond, hitting old haunts that were now "our" places.

But, honestly, I knew from the beginning Marcus was The One. On our first date, back when I first ar-rived at my housesit in Kent, we decided to meet at a Polish restaurant in South Kensington, giving each other a half-hour window because we were both com-ing from outside the city. While we were on the phone, he researched which train I'd catch; it would take an hour.

Date morning dawned bright and crisp. I left two hours early, just in case. Delays started immediately: I couldn't figure out how to lock the front door. (What is it with British locks?) Finally tamed tricky lock; twenty minutes wasted. Took wrong turn driving to the train station; thirty minutes shot. Missed my train; another fifteen minutes until the next one. Cellphone died en route and I couldn't access Marcus's number. Tube into South Ken was running behind. I burst into the restaurant, an hour and a half late, disheveled, flushed from hot flashes; all heads turned toward me.

And there was Marcus, calmly sipping a glass of wine. "I'm so, so sorry," I gushed slipping into the chair opposite him. He ordered me a glass of wine.

"I'm really sorry," I started to relay my saga.

He looked at me and quietly interrupted, "I knew you'd come."

I breathed deeply and smiled. "And I knew you'd still be here."

Chapter 13

OMG, WHAT HAVE I GOTTEN MYSELF INTO?

AT SOME POINT BEFORE your housesit, in spite of all the self-awareness, research and gut-checking, you might get nervous. Someone close to you might plant a seed of doubt by exclaiming, "You're doing what?!" Or you might get a bit overwhelmed by the travel preparations. Or you might experience what I call pre-trip heebie-jeebies about your destination. After eight years, this still happens to me sometimes. Here are some tips I've learned to deal with my pre-trip jitters:

Remind myself this is normal! Traveling to a place or situation that is unknown is both nerve-wracking and exciting in its uncertainty. By reminding myself of travel's challenges and opportunities, I can rise above my anxieties and fears.

Create a "support network" back home. Before I go, I enlist friends and family to engage with me on social media, send me email updates from home or be available for phone or Skype calls.

Post on housesitting Facebook groups my upcoming sitting assignment to see if there are other housesitters with whom I might meet up.

Update my communication technology by downloading mobile phone apps such as What's App or installing Skype on my laptop.

Buy tickets to a cultural or sporting event before my trip to have something tangible to anticipate.

Subscribe to emails from www.TimeOut.com or www.GroupOn.com to learn about discounted events and services (such as dance lessons) that get me excited about my destination.

Research MeetUp or expat groups and engage with their leaders beforehand. This helps create a sense of community before I even arrive. For example, I often find writers groups through Meet-Up so I have ready-made "friends" and an activity to go to at my new location. Or, I join a Facebook group of locals. You never know what you will stumble across: While researching Facebook for groups in Dakar, Senegal, prior to a housesit there, I found an acquaintance's posts from a few years ago! I emailed him and he introduced me via email to local friends.

Ask my homeowners to introduce me to some of their friends, or to suggest activities I might like.

For example, one of my favorite homeowners, knowing of my interest in helping refugees, sent me a link to a local woman who was raising awareness about refugees in Berlin through a unique walking tour called "Refugee Voices." Although I'd been to Berlin several times before, this was a welcome — and thoughtful — introduction at a repeat sitting assignment...and the tour guide and I became friends!

Post my travel plans on my own social media (taking care not to provide too many details that might expose my home to vandals). Once, I was looking for contacts in Nagasaki, Japan, and was introduced via a friend of a Facebook "friend" to a woman who hosted me during the city's 70th commemoration of the atomic bombing.

Remember "this too shall pass." Reminding myself that I can do anything for a week, or two, or three, relieves some of my pre-trip butterflies and helps me focus instead on the adventure of it all!

> 🐾 INSIDER TIP: A great resource for in-person social events reflecting interests that range from cocktail meet-and-greets to hiking groups is www.InterNations.org. It's free to join and there are forums for posting questions. 🐾

🐾 HOT! INSIDER TIP: www.MapaHub.com is a new website for registered house-sitter/members to "pin" on a world map their sitting assign-ments and dates. It's a great way to connect IRL ("in real life") with other fascinating housesitters. And nothing beats the blues like meeting other housesitters! 🐾

Chapter 14

OK, I'M HERE!
NOW WHAT?

NOW THAT YOU'VE ARRIVED, perhaps jet-lagged, it's important to continue to act as if you are on a job interview. After all, you want the homeowners to leave home feeling confident they made the perfect choice in a sitter! Carry a notebook to record all pet and home instructions, and specifically ask about things they might not think to show you.

Here's the checklist I use so I don't forget anything:

√ Fuse box location.

√ Location of water shut-off valves.

√ Location of flashlights and extra batteries for TV/DVD remotes.

√ Landline phone and instructions for dialing, including dialing the emergency number (fire department, police and ambulance), and dialing the emergency veterinarian. It's not always straightforward. In Mexico, for example, local numbers are dialed with one prefix if you are dialing from a landline, and another if you are dialing from a mobile.

√ Clothes washer, clothes dryer and dishwasher instructions.

√ Instructions for using the shower, if it's foreign to you.

√ Location and instructions for setting/disarming any alarms, nanny-cams or other security system.

√ Instructions for using the TV, DVD, Netflix, etc. and remotes.

√ Test locking and unlocking all doors — from both the inside and the outside.

√ Test-drive the car and lock and unlock it.

√ Internet modem location.

√ Location of things not to touch or eat.

√ Place where trash and recycling are collected.

√ Allowable parking places.

√ Contact info for household help (housekeepers, gardeners, pool maintenance). Check pay envelopes.

√ Most homeowners leave an envelope with cash for emergencies. If used, be sure to leave receipts and an accurate accounting of money spent.

√ If you have time, ask to be shown the locations of the nearest grocery store, pharmacy, health clinic, and taxi, bus or metro stop.

√ Ask to meet a neighbor or trusted friend.

√ Enter into your cellphone the phone numbers for the veterinarian and the friend with the extra key.

√ Location of extra bed linens, so you can leave a fresh bed.

Of course, interact with the pets and watch how the homeowners interact with them.

🐾 INSIDER TIP: Typically, the homeowners will treat you to a welcome dinner at their home or a local restaurant. Behave! You are still on a job interview! 🐾

Chapter 15

LIVING ON TOP OF OTHER PEOPLE'S STUFF

KEEPING TRACK OF YOUR STUFF is trickier when you are living on top of someone else's stuff. Some homeowners will clear space in a closet or dresser, but others may not have the room. So, this is your chance to get creative. Here are my tips:

As you settle in, find one place where you will always put the keys when you enter. It might be in the door lock (if it can't be accessed from the outside), or in a bowl on a shelf near the door. The, um, key is to find a place that is intuitive and easy where you will automatically drop the keys upon entering.

I find *one* hiding place for my passport, credit cards and other valuables and one consistent place where I hide my laptop — every time I go out.

If you are a chronic cellphone and key misplacer, you might want to invest in a Bluetooth tracker. These little devices (such as Qwer and Tile Mate) slide onto your key ring or into your wallet or suitcase. Misplaced valuables are found by pressing a search button on an app that activates the device's beeping sound and shows the last location of your valuable on a map. (How's that for tracking lost luggage?) Press the button on the device and your misplaced cellphone rings.

Even on long housesits, I limit my "living" to certain spaces in the house so my belongings and work aren't spread around.

I find one place to unpack where I keep all my clothes together. At one housesitting assignment in a cramped terrace house in London, I used the baby's crib as my "dresser."

Ditto for the kitchen: I keep all my dry goods in one space and arrange my refrigerated stuff in a single compact area.

Bathrooms can pose the biggest challenge, as they are usually small and already cluttered. For shorter sits, I have a small travel bag with pockets that hangs over a towel hook. This is where I easily keep my toiletries and toothbrush.

For longer sits, I buy one of those over-the-door hanging storage thingies that has plastic pockets meant for shoes and hang it over the back of the bathroom door. This becomes my medicine cabinet where I can stow a hair dryer, toiletries, medicines, needle and thread, etc. I put my "office" stuff in these pockets, too. They usually cost only a few dollars and I leave them behind. When I leave my recurring housesit in Mexico, I roll it up and store it in a closet with my vitamins, shampoo and cold medicines all ready for me when I return.

I put a cup in the bathroom for my jewelry, and it's where my rings and necklaces always go. I use a cup because it's tougher for curious cats to get into.

Computer and phone cables are easily left behind, so I proactively focus on where I plug them in. I charge my phone in the bathroom and leave it on the counter near the sink where it is visible and less likely to be forgotten. I use only one outlet for my computer cord. Exception: Bunny sits. Computer, phone and other nibbly-tempting cords go up on a shelf — one shelf — and stay there!

Some housesitters take extensive photos of how the house looks when they arrive before they move the homeowners' belongings to accommodate themselves and their own stuff. When they prepare to leave, they return the kitchen cupboards, fridge, bathroom and elsewhere back to the original states.

One of my first purchases when I arrive is hydrogen peroxide to keep on hand for emergencies. I use it as a topical antibiotic, a dental cleanser, and a de-skunker.

(Mix 1 quart hydrogen peroxide, ¼ cup baking soda, and 1 teaspoon dishwashing liquid. Wearing gloves, apply liberally to area hit by the skunk, rubbing the mixture through the fur down to the skin. Let stand about 20 minutes and rinse. Repeat, if necessary.)

To absorb lingering smoke smells, place around bowls of vinegar.

I always carry binder clips, the office supply that is usually used for securing stacks of papers. They: Pin up clothes for drying, pinch bags tight, temporarily (or longer!) repair a torn hem or busted luggage strap, hold electronic cords neatly, tightly close recalcitrant shower curtains, and, of course, keep all my papers organized. They do anything that duct tape, clothespins, those baggie clip thingies, or safety pins do ...and more.

> 🐾 INSIDER TIP: I wait to unpack until I'm rested. I unpack with intention, really focusing on my task and paying attention to where I put my things. I leave my belongings out in plain sight, so as I pack to leave, I can easily scan the house for my stuff. 🐾

Chapter 16

LEAVING A GREAT IMPRESSION

NOW THAT THE HOUSESITTING assignment is over, you want to leave a great impression. Here's a list of things to consider two or three days before the home-owners return:

Start consolidating your things into two or three contained areas, so you don't leave anything behind that the homeowners will need to mail to you.

Restock food, cleaning materials and paper products.

Make or buy a "welcome home" meal, perhaps including a bottle of wine or coffee (depending on the time of day of the homeowners' return).

Schedule your time to clean the house and launder the sheets. This can be tricky if you have a morning departure. You'll want to leave a clean bed, but that might mean leaving behind used sheets and towels in the clothes washer. Be sure to discuss this with the homeowners ahead of time, so they aren't surprised to return to dirty laundry. You will not want to leave the house with either the washer or the dryer running.

Email the homeowners to confirm their return time, confirm your departure, ask if there's anything special they'd like upon their return, and, of course, to thank them!

Some housesitters leave a small gift — a photo of the pet, perhaps — as a token of thanks.

Even if you will be seeing them when they return, prepare a brief note of anything noteworthy that occurred: Phone messages, package deliveries, breakage, unusual pet behavior. They will likely be jet-lagged and travel-weary, so a brief written synopsis will give them time to digest the information at their convenience.

Some housesitters take photos or videos of the home if they leave before the homeowners' return. This gives them a record in case the homeowners have any concerns.

Be aware of not overdoing it. If you go overboard with cleaning, for example, or with training the dog, some homeowners might feel as if they'd been judged negatively. You want them to feel great about arriving to the same place they left — their home and pets.

🐾 INSIDER TIP: Pay attention to the homeowners' return energy. Consider how far they had to travel, how many time zones they traversed, whether they left beloved grandchildren and might be a bit blue. You know how obnoxious it is when someone is "on" when you aren't? This is an important time to show sensitivity. 🐾

Chapter 17

GETTING ASKED BACK

THE HOLY GRAIL of housesitting is getting asked back to sitting assignments that you loved. I've turned down repeat requests for a variety of reasons: Most often, the timing of the repeat sit didn't work for me. Sometimes, the location just wasn't right for me.

Once, I turned down a coveted location because I felt uncomfortable with how the homeowners reacted when they returned home. (I'd knocked myself out, but they still complained — about things, it turned out, that weren't true. For example, they complained I hadn't locked their car after I'd started it for them, when I had manually locked it. Since their remote needed to be engaged twice, they'd concluded I'd left their car unlocked.) My relationship with these homeowners didn't feel good, so I politely declined future offers.

But, my most soul-fulfilling housesits have been with homeowners and pets I *did* feel great about. Here's how I helped create those relationships:

The relationship with the homeowners, of course, starts before the housesit. Be honest, be vulnerable, be personable, be empathetic. One of my very favorite repeat housesits in London was initially to care for an older cat and a kitten. When the homeowners emailed that the kitten had been killed on the road just weeks before my arrival, I sent condolence flowers to the older kitty. The homeowners were quite appreciative of my empathizing with their loss. Since then, we've become best of friends.

Although I provide a great service to the home-owners, I never forget how kind they are to allow me into their home to care for their most honored family members. Gratitude goes a long way to cement a long-term relationship!

I maintain relationships after my housesitting as-signments. Usually, my homeowners and I "friend" each other on Facebook, and I continue to check their feeds to comment on the pets I've cared for. As I would with any beloved friend, I send notes at holiday times wishing them well. Many times, they've referred me to neighbors or co-workers.

When I'm housesitting in a location I love, I make a point of meeting neighbors and other pet owners. I give out my email address at dog parks and I talk up what I do. I gather email addresses from interested pet owners — and follow up.

When it's time to leave, I don't linger. Some sitters stay after the housesitting assignment has ended, but I think that can be confusing for the pets, as well as intrusive to the homeowners.

Finally, don't judge the homeowners — not for their housekeeping (or lack thereof), not for their pet training (or lack thereof), not for their way of life. Your job is to keep their routine going smoothly — not to "improve." I heard of one couple housesitting in a Third World country who felt the household help was underpaid, so they increased wages. Imagine the problems that caused for the homeowner when he returned! Homeowners trust you to care for their home and pets — not to make them feel bad about their lives.

> 🐾 INSIDER TIP: When homeowners return to a clean home the way they left it, and their pets are calm and relaxed, you are sure to lead their list of housesitters next time they travel! 🐾

BETWEEN THE LINES

WHILE HOUSESITTING in a "small village" of 1.5 million people in China, I was the only non-western face I saw in over a week.

I relied on communicating through Google-translating phrases on my laptop such as "minibus to panda sanctuary" and photographing the Chinese letters with my cellphone to show to taxi and minibus drivers.

I always got to my destination, but the Chinese equivalent of online translating seemed lacking…

While on a minibus, for example, a young Chinese woman spoke into her cellphone and handed it down the line of passengers to me.

"Are you a man needs parts?" the phone read.

Ummmm. I shrugged in confusion and handed the phone back down the line to her.

She spoke again into her phone and passed it to me.

"Are you a man needs parts?"

After thinking for a minute, I ventured, "Yes, I'm American."

She nodded and smiled.

Chapter 18

WHEN THINGS GO WRONG

...AND THEY WILL! That's why you are there. After all, if life were entirely predictable, there'd be no reason to have a housesitter!

Things will go wrong with the house: A leak, a broken window. That's why you've earlier secured the names of repair people.

Things will go wrong with the pets: That's why you have the pet's veterinarian info and the emergency vet info handy. If you are a member of www.Trusted-Housesitters.com, you can also contact the site's 24/7 veterinarian for advice.

Things may go wrong with you: That's why you've secured the local medical clinic info and the name of someone to take over for you in an emergency. Hopefully, you've secured a multi-entry visa to ease your return in case you need to leave the country in an emergency.

Other things may go wrong. It's just smart to have resources for a Plan B if the homeowners cancel on you — which is really inconsiderate. If you have to cancel on them because of a dire emergency, it's wise — and professional — to help them find a replacement. You can post on closed housesit Facebook groups such as HouseSittingCafe (my favorite) or HouseSittingWorld.

If the housesit is not as you anticipated and you are not happy, you have two options: suck it up and learn what to ask future homeowners, or leave, which I find really unprofessional. Breaking your commitment reflects badly on the rest of us housesitters — and might get you banned from some of the housesitting platforms.

Sometimes, travel plans create unforeseen glitches. The homeowners' local emergency friend can be invaluable during these times.

> 🐾 INSIDER TIP: If the home-owners cross the International Date Line, ask them to double-check the actual day they return home. 🐾

NOT *THAT* KIND OF BUZZED

HOUSESITTING IN MEXICO provides all kinds of opportunities to increase my vocabulary. A recent *palabra du jour*, for example, was: *avispa*.

Meaning "wasp" — and not the non-Jewish type — the word buzzed into my vocabulary when I saw several of the furry flyers building a huge, unpermitted wasp-condo complex, maybe even a multiplex with underground parking and an open-air amphitheater, on the ceiling of my beloved "happy hour" patio where I housesit. The swarm was three or four wasps deep with several dozen/hundred/thousand condo-dwelling wannabes ("wanna bees," get it?) milling around.

Not sure how to handle this hive, I emailed a guy who used to broker stocks, herd sheep, and keep bees who now wrangles writers. He suggested I call the fire department because with everything built in adobe, the firefighters get bored and will de-bee for free.

No one at the *bombero* station spoke English, so I blurted over the phone, *"Tengo un problema con avispas,"* hissing the last word as if I were talking about underworld spies or drug kingpins. The fireman promised to be out shortly (I think, this was all in Spanish over the telephone), which then lent itself to the great existential question: What does one wear to a dewasping?

I expected hoses and hatchets, but it was all very simple: The hooded, gloved, cloaked *bombero* sprayed water and soap all over the layers of wasps, causing mass carnage and consternation. He used dishwashing soap; you know, the kind Madge used to soak fingernails in? He then scooped gobs of soggy wasps into a Wal-Mart plastic bag and went on his way, promising to return the next day to show any renegade wasps who's their daddy.

At another housesitting gig, I increased my vocabulary even further. Here's what the week looked like:

Sunday: Padded barefoot, carrying my shoes, to the downstairs bedroom and made an almost intimate acquaintance with a very black scorpion on the bright white floor. Beat to death with shoe. May have dented the ceramic tiles in my enthusiasm. Vowed to watch every step I take. Learned *alacran*.

Tuesday: Learned *serpiente de cascabel*. "Cascabel" is a word I actually know from my first grade rendition of "Jingle Bells": *Cascabel, cascabel, musica de amor...*

So, it never occurred to me that such a benign, jolly word would cause the four rescue dogs I was watching to raise such a ruckus out in the yard. When I went to investigate, I could hear the snake's rattle all the way across the yard (though I didn't know what it was, since I'd never before heard an angry *serpiente de cascabel*).

It was a *¡muy grande* serpiente!*

I didn't know what to do, so I started throwing things at the snake — anything I could find — golf balls, an empty Coke can — hoping it would slither off. Instead, it reared its head, daring me to come closer. Finally, I remembered there was a meat cleaver in the kitchen. Looking like a version of Jack Nicholson in *The Shining*, I heaved the cleaver and missed the snake by a mile. It sneered. I did have the garden hose coiled at my feet, but the snake was strikingly close to the spigot. It stuck out its tongue at me.

So, another S.O.S. call to *los guapos bomberos*. I stuck the dogs inside and waited on the road for the firemen. Five uniformed guys in their twenties and one young woman who looked like a girlfriend tag-along arrived carrying baseball bats, a long metal pole, gardening gloves and one blackened fire jacket. By the time they set up camp, the snake had *adiosed*. The young fire-fighters spent half an hour literally beating the bushes to flush out the snake. Defeated, they told me to call them when it returns.

Returns?

Wednesday: One of the dogs killed a squirrel and made a big show of it in the backyard. (Don't squirrels carry bubonic plague?) Unable to deal with the lifeless beady eyes, I covered the corpse with a bucket, guiltily leaving it for the gardener to deal with. Learned *ardilla*. *Ardilla muerta*.

Friday: After a delightful afternoon sharing wine with a friend and a relaxing evening watching a favorite movie, I headed downstairs to go to bed. In the bathroom, I started to brush my teeth when I saw — and I swear I am not exaggerating — a three-inch scorpion crawling in the sink!

Luckily, I prefer my dangerous and gross predators in the sink because I don't have to resort to *mano-a-mano* combat. I flipped up the spigot and started scooping water over the scorpion. Its milky white tail reared, but it didn't flush. Finally, I created a personal Niagara Falls that doomed it down the drain. I triumphantly spat toothpaste in its wake.

Relaxed once more, I continued brushing my teeth, keeping the spigot running full-force, just to be sure. Then, like from a Japanese horror film, I saw first one, then more, scorpion elbows emerge from the drain, hoisting the reincarnated arachnid back into my sink.

Now I freaked. The hand soap wouldn't squirt fast enough; I grabbed a bottle of shampoo and doused it, praying it would die a well-coifed death.

So just why do I housesit in Mexico?

Well, it's not just the critters that crawl; time does, too. I spent a lovely day recently with a dear friend, whom I met at noon to do "something." When I arrived at her place, she offered to make us sandwiches for lunch and announced she was making chicken enchiladas for dinner. Nine hours later, belly and heart more than full, I headed home. When was the last time I spent nine hours with a friend just hanging out and chatting? There's a lot to be said for savoring.

Learned *muy contenta*.

Chapter 19

SHHHH! 3 SECRET TIPS

HERE ARE MY SUPER-SECRET tips for landing great housesits:

SECRET TIP #1: Write a dynamic introduction letter that really describes who you are, even if it might be controversial. For example, I write upfront that I'm writing a book about my experiences in the Middle East with Iraqi and Palestinian refugees. Only once (that I know of) has that turned off a homeowner: A former British bomber pilot who decided to take the opportunity to dress me down for being a peace advocate. We probably would not have been a good match.

On the other hand, my political work has definitely pushed me to the top of some homeowners' short-lists. Not that I need to sit for homeowners who agree with me politically, but my passion makes me more "real" when I express it honestly and openly.

When I've interviewed potential sitters to care for my home in Santa Monica, CA, the ones who have stood out described (briefly) their spiritual paths, or their commitment to travel blogging, or their online teaching, or something else that made their personality stand out from the rest of the pack.

So, my advice is: Be bold and be honest!

SECRET TIP #2: Apply for sitting assignments you'd like in the future, even if the dates don't match. For example, I decided I wanted to spend a summer in Vietnam, so I applied for a housesit in Hanoi that was listed for February explaining that I wasn't available then, but would be the next summer.

The homeowner responded asking me if I'd Skype with her fifth-grade students to talk about my experiences with refugees. So, from my housesit in Mexico, I Skyped with her class in Hanoi. It was a great experience! As you can imagine, when the homeowner was ready to make her summer travel plans, I was at the top of the list (she never even posted the assignment) and I spent an incredible six weeks in Hanoi spoiling Brody, the sweetest labrador puppy around.

This doesn't guarantee anything, of course, but it's a way to start building relationships. I've developed friendships with homeowners for whom I've never housesat (yet!).

SECRET TIP #3: Join housesitting groups on social media and participate. I like HouseSittingCafe Facebook group. I post tips, offer suggestions when asked, and follow the travels of certain friends. I also post where I'm sitting — and hoping to sit. Not only have I been referred housesitting assignments from my Facebook peeps, I've met up with other housesitters in real life and created some lovely friendships. More than once, my Facebook peeps have made introductions to their own friends in cities where I'm housesitting.

Chapter 20

BONUS FOR HOMEOWNERS: HOW TO HOUSESITTER-PROOF YOUR HOME

NOTHING MAKES A HOUSESIT great like clear boundaries and communication. At a new housesit, I appreciate when the homeowners:

Store away anything they don't want me to touch and any belongings that would break their hearts if they broke.

Lock up anything that would compromise the security of their identity. While couch surfing, I once stayed in a woman's office — where she had all of her passwords taped to the wall!

Are clear about guests. I ask ahead of time, of course. I'm not talking about picking up strangers on the metro. But I do occasionally meet up with friends and it's nice to invite them back for a cup of tea.

Are honest with themselves about having a virtual stranger stay in their home. When homeowners are appreciative of my presence, I am more comfortable being there.

Chapter 21

ANOTHER BONUS FOR HOMEOWNERS: 10 WAYS YOU CAN WELCOME YOUR NEW HOUSESITTER

AFTER A HOUSESITTER has paid to travel to your community, committed him/herself to staying in your home and taken on the responsibility of caring for your pets, it's wonderful if you can truly make the sitter feel "at home." Here are ten ways you can welcome your housesitter:

Arrange an airport pickup if your housesitter is flying from a long distance and won't have easy transportation to your home. Or meet him/her at the closest public transportation stop to help with luggage.

Provide adequate supplies of paper goods (e.g., toilet paper, paper towels) and cleaning supplies.

Have some starter food or meals prepared. It's such a treat for a housesitter to not have to grocery shop right after a long flight or drive. Usually, homeowners treat their sitters to a nice meal to welcome them.

Clear some space in the closet, dresser, bathroom and refrigerator.

Clean as you would for a houseguest, or spring for a cleaning service before your sitter arrives. Nothing says "thank you" like a clean home!

Provide adequate supplies of pet food, kitty litter, treats, medicine and any other pet-related needs.

Introduce your sitter to a friend who might be interested in sharing a meal or a sightseeing adventure. Some homeowners have invited their "emergency contact" friend along during the "welcome dinner."

Leave a list of nearby restaurants — perhaps fliers with menus.

Provide clear and complete instructions for the TV, DVD, and Netflix.

Provide a local map showing favorite walks, great restaurants and public transportation stops.

Chapter 22

A FINAL NOTE

THANKS FOR JOINING ME on my journey! For me, housesitting has opened a whole new world — in many ways. I hope you find this book helpful — whether you are a seasoned sitter or someone starting out. I'd love your feedback. Email me directly at Kelly@LivingLargeInLimbo.com.

Mosey on by www.BecomeAHousesitter.com to drop me a note about your sitting experiences, tips and questions. Perhaps you'd like to submit a blog?

Happy Housesitting!

ACKNOWLEDGMENTS

EVEN A SIMPLE BOOK like this takes a village! Hearty thanks to David Pisarra, who nagged me for ages to write this book, to Ian Usher for his fabulous website design and publishing and marketing advice, to Maria Atkins of CatMadSitters for her incredible research and to Sally Asante, whose eagle-sharp eye snatched a couple more typos.

Thank you to the many early readers who provided insights and inspiration. Special thanks to Ken Bridges, Tracy McDermott and Vanessa Anderson for such thorough comments.

Thanks to all the homeowners who've been generous enough to share their homes and beloved pets with me; I am humbled. Special thanks to Barbara and Delaine Mountain for making me feel like special family at their home in Mexico, where I am privileged to spoil ChaCha every spring and fall.

And thanks to Marcus Usherwood, who lives in my heart and is my "home," no matter where I am in the world.

SEEN IN

AARP'S "LIFE REIMAGINED" SERIES
The Gig Economy — Making It Work for You
www.lifereimagined.aarp.org/page/both/40039-The--Gig-Economy----Making-it-Work-for-You

The gig economy's tradeoffs are outweighed by the advantages, she says. "My expenses are a fraction of what they were when I had my fulltime office and staff. I live on less, but overall I'm netting slightly more. I have a lot less security, but I've learned to live with a greater level of faith. My life is richer and more fulfilling than when I was tethered to a desk."

CREDITCARDS.COM
You Did WHAT To Pay Off Your Debt?
www.creditcards.com/credit-card-news/you-did-what-pay-off-debt-1266.php

"It took about 10 years to pay off all my debt," says Hayes-Raitt, "and you know what? Turns out the 'extremes' weren't so extreme. I fell into a lifestyle I prefer. My life is simpler now. I have a chance to live a life I'd always dreamed of. I now housesit around the world. This summer, I was in Malaysia for nine weeks and Japan for two. And I have a [newspaper] column I enjoy writing for which I am paid."

MARKETWATCH.COM and THEMONEYSTREET.COM

Rent A Mansion This Summer — For Your Dog
www.marketwatch.com/story/4-ways-to-plan-your-dogs-summer-vacation-2014-05-22

"I live in the pets' homes in exchange for a free opportunity to explore a new community," she says. Since 2009, she says she's lived in 14 different homes (some repeatedly) and taken care of the homeowners' pets.

LEARNVEST.COM and NORTHWESTERNMUTUAL.COM

People Share the Savvy Ways They Swap Skills and Services
www.learnvest.com/2015/07/barter-sites-and-services/3/

"I've lived in London for two months during the Olympics; in a glorious, four-story home with panoramic views of Lake Chapala in Mexico; and in a funky country home across from a rice paddy in Langkawi, Malaysia."

ABOUT THE AUTHOR

KELLY HAYES-RAITT ADMITS that she sleeps around to finance the book she's writing about her experiences working in the Middle East with refugees.

Ten years ago, after a 30-year career as a political activist promoting social and environmental justice, Kelly ran for public office and got her butt kicked. She decided to take a sabbatical from politics and visited the Middle East several times. She ended up working with refugees.

To finance her writing, she rents out her own home and lives elsewhere by housesitting. She's been house-sitting fulltime since 2009 in the U.S., Mexico, the U.K., Germany, Denmark, the Netherlands, Gibraltar, Vietnam, Cambodia, China, Singapore, Japan, Malaysia, Senegal, Malawi and Mozambique. She's visited more than 60 countries, including pre- and post-U.S. invasion Iraq and has co-led delegations in Syria and India.

She's an inspiring and engaging public speaker who loves to share her experiences. Her audiences have included Congresswomen in the U.S. Capitol who acted upon her reports from Iraq and activists in Poland, Mexico, the Philippines and the West Bank.

Chapters in Kelly's forthcoming refugee book are included in seven anthologies and have won 19 literary awards. She writes a column about social justice issues for a Los Angeles weekly newspaper. The column was awarded "second place" by the Southern California Journalists Association in 2016.

To hear Kelly read the award-winning essay about meeting an Iraqi beggar just days before the U.S.-led invasion of Iraq — and finding her again three months after the occupation of Baghdad — visit www.Living-LargeInLimbo.com.

And check out her political and public relations bio at www.LivingLargeInLimbo.com/about.

Kelly is available for interviews and presentations live or taped via Skype to school classes, book clubs, podcasts and media programs anywhere in the world. She is also available to speak at conferences. And, of course, she'd love to talk with you about spoiling your pets!

Besides sleeping around with animals, Kelly is an avid scuba diver who strives to perfect her octopus-whispering.

Find her at Kelly@LivingLargeInLimbo.com.

COMING SOON!

...TO A BOOK CLUB, RADIO SHOW or convention near you. To schedule Kelly, contact her at Kelly@-LivingLargeInLimbo.com or check out her website at www.HouseSitDiva.com.

Next up: *How to Find the Right Housesitter*, a book for homeowners searching for the right housesitter. Follow www.FindTheRightHousesitter.com for updates.

In the works: *Living Large In Limbo: How I Found Myself Among the World's Forgotten*, Kelly's book of journalistic essays about her experiences in Iraq, Syria and Lebanon working with refugees. Stalk www.LivingLargeInLimbo.com for details, as well as for a download of Kelly reading the book's award-winning chapter about her encounter with an Iraqi beggar girl.

Sign up at www.LivingLargeInLimbo.com for free to stay connected with Kelly.

Made in the USA
Middletown, DE
14 March 2018